The Labradorable Tails

The woof guide to
master muttlery

This book is dedicated to
Simon, my rock
&
My Staunton family in Snugborough

Acknowledgements:
Pamela Gray for capturing my spark. Conal Finnerty, my Supervet star. Judith Cheetham, chew sticks and reading bits. John Maguire MC at MCC. Barry Murphy, graphic design guru. Rob Reid let this dog see the rabbit. Sharon Keating for karma. Stephanie Garret and Sparkle. Phil Lee for reading me in the rough. My Staunton home and Snugborough's Snugglers. The coolest Cloonee Cuddlers. Patsy and Liam. Mary Lally. Castlebar Family Markets and Pet World at Horkans. Momo Heneghan and Mixed Up Cat With Lines On. Simon, sweet soul mate and mud brother.

© Rosie Lowe 2016

ISBN: 9780995796713

Illustrations by
Pamela Gray

Contents

The General Prodogue 5

The Introchucktion 7

The Summoned Tail 9

The Reprieve's Tail 11

The Fryer Tuck's Tail 13

The Hip Man's Tail 15

The Wind Up Merchant's Tail 17

The Bark's Tail 19

The Squire's Tail 21

The Postmistress's Tail 23

The Knight's Tail 25

The Man of Paw's Tail 27

The Ploughman's Tail 29

The Why The Bath? Tail 31

The Parson's Nose Tail 33

The Honk's Tail 35

The Physician's Tail 37

The Pardon Me Tail 39

The Cook's Tail 41

The Manhandled Tail 43

The Miller's Tail 45

The Frankincense's Tail 47

The Bin Beast's Tail 49

The Man of Love's Tail 51

Epidogue 53

The General Prodogue

Welcome to The Labradorable Tails
Of my life's story I shall for you regale
Flew down from Heaven on black velvet wings
To love, to hug & show the joy of all things
I began my journey in Castlebar
In Mayo, Ireland I voiced my first bark
October nineteenth nineteen ninety-eight
An auspicious date I could hardly wait
These tails I'll tell you to tally twenty-two
My name is Chuck and I'm pleased to meet you
So for what is what and who is who
Let us begin without further ado

Introchucktion

Labradorable me with a spring in my step
Bounded through life loving all whom I met
Brown eyed, bushy tailed with baritone bark
Summersaults of joy when taken for walks
Rooting in ditches, oh glorious mud!
Scent of a pheasant, sleuth like to the woods
Duck hunts with the lads in my formative years
Running, tongue lolling, hot breath, flapping ears
Trained to scent & retrieve, a much-prized dog
Hunter-gatherer so I was, so I was
My bed, a treasure trove, oh sacred of spaces
Odd sods of turf, stale bread, old suitcases

My purpose in life was to make the world smile
With clumsy clown hugs & big raised high fives
Talking to all with my own Chuck speak
Eyebrow number, jerk of head, bark & squeak
Tall dark & handsome both inside and out
The ladies all swooned when I was about
This gentleman giant carried handbags in
Groceries from car boots hung from my chin
Watched over Eileen when the funeral was done
Kissed away tears as she mourned for her mum
Tails to enchant you with my life & times
Let's traverse as pilgrims on this path of rhyme

The Summoned Tail

An 18th Birthday gift was I to be
October birth brothers, Darragh Staunton & me
It was I who chose my Master you see
Waddled up to his heart & turned the key
Summoned to Snugborough in a few weeks time
Pick of the litter, my soul swelled with pride
Christmas games with my sisters & brothers
Roll over play fights & winding up mother
Gannet-like greed had me top of the class
First in the food chain & cutting a dash
A shining black diamond puppy in bloom
Every head turned when I entered the room

January came & then I was ready
Leaving the nest, my excitement heady
Chauffer driven to my brand new abode
Warm in the basement & "Home Sweet Home"
Nestled down to Eileen's bedtime stories
Swaddled & snuggled, settled & cosy
My waking hours proved a walk on the wild side
Puppy years were a roller coaster ride
Designer jeans & silk shirts were all mine
Devouring shoes & ravaging clotheslines
Only stopping for breath when suppertime came
Steak pie & gravy had this muck savage tamed

Welcomed into the family, what luck for this pup
I was christened Chuck their bonny young buck
My cuddles were legend & talk of the town
This Snugborough Snuggler hugged away frowns
Darragh, Ronan, Fintan & Eileen
My pack to watch over, ears sharp & eyes keen
Of my peepers vets had never before seen
Soul windows as perfect, pure gold & pristine
Lit from within with a fire & a grace
Mercurial flash of an angel's face
Summoned to journey with earthly mortals
Viewed through my soft velvet brown portals

The Reprieve's Tail

Forgive me your honour for I have sinned
Burying handbags & rooting through bins
Spanish leather shoes of Eileen's were pinched
Returned a year later, pure jovial high jinx
Ecco shoes I destroyed, Fintan's pride & joy
Sent outside in shame a scolded bold boy
Fine foodstuffs snaffled by man's own best fiend
Swivel of snout as I licked all plates clean
Wanderlust took over me many a time
King of the bog land, the world was all mine
Missing in action for days upon end
Running with vagabonds my new best friends

My basement lair was a hotbed of crime
Contraband goods stashed of every kind
Milk cartons, watches & huge wads of cash
House bricks & mobiles gone in a flash
Children's toys, clothes pegs, old shortbread tins
Crisp packets, beer cans & rusted mattress springs
Car keys, autumn leaves, Master Card & Visa
Magpie-like swoop of a real diamond geezer
Pilfering shopping bags, head in the freezer
Mauled marzipan & the missing Maltesers
The lightest of chocolate lifted so easy
Puppy Enemy Number One just got too greedy

Labrador Reliever of man's worldly goods
Crime spree as long as a mafia hood
The Dogfather me, a real Al Capbone
Mad, lab & dangerous to know
After supper, living high on the hog
Post- dinner lie down, an unsuspecting dog
Darragh with SWAT team, search warrant signed
Evicted, frisked, house arrest & a fine
Nicked & nabbed by the long arm of the law
Had me banged to rights with four handcuffed paws
Swag confiscated, the guilt was all mine
But for Eileen's reprieve, I'd have done time

The Fryer Tuck's Tail

The way to a dog's heart is through his tum
All manner of tasty treats, yummy yum yum
The finest of sounds to reach these dog-ears
Tin opener on food tins, Heaven was here
Chew sticks, rashers, roast beef, Yorkshire puds
Getting one's gnashers round a roasted spud
Tucked into Eileen's bacon & cabbage
Lamb with mint sauce had tail in full waggage
Ploughed through platefuls of chicken and chips
Haunting the kitchen whilst licking my lips
Bear hugged the oven, my favourite place
The source of the smile on this well-fed face

Loitering with intent on baking day
Intoxicating smells as I sat and prayed
Through the cooking glass rose wonderful things
Soda bread, currant scones, fruitcake was King
Cottage loaves, fairy cakes, fluffy jam sponge
On the top shelf very hot & cross buns
I had my chops round that lot sooner or later
The undisputed all you could eat baker
My mega bite mouth had that oven cleaned
I ate for all Ireland, became broad at the beam
Acute sense of smell, well qualified to judge
I was Gordon Gecko & greed was good

Full Irish Breakfast each Sunday I sighed
Ritual family banquet, the fry
I gazed in awe at the goodies displayed
Plump pink pork sausages sizzled & sprayed
Streaks of back bacon flashed hot & turned crisp
Baked beans bubbled, potato cakes hissed
Fried beef tomatoes tar sticky, browns hashed
Golden yolks erupting in molten spit spat
Simmertime & the liver fried easy
Kippers jumpin' & the hotpots hissed high
Your dog was rich on his mammy's good cookin'
Hushed Chucky baby as he downed his fry

The Hip Man's Tail

A new age man of the world was I
Alternative therapies opened my eyes
In more ways than one I was always on trend
Introduced to Philip, my new best friend
He marvelled at this magnificent physique
Prescribed full body massage to stay at my peak
Consent was given, so delighted was I
A hip man dude & a real fly guy
For an hour each day I was well away
Eased muscle tension, kept arthritis at bay
Eyes closed to the sounds of the radio
Sound as a pound pummelled from head to toe

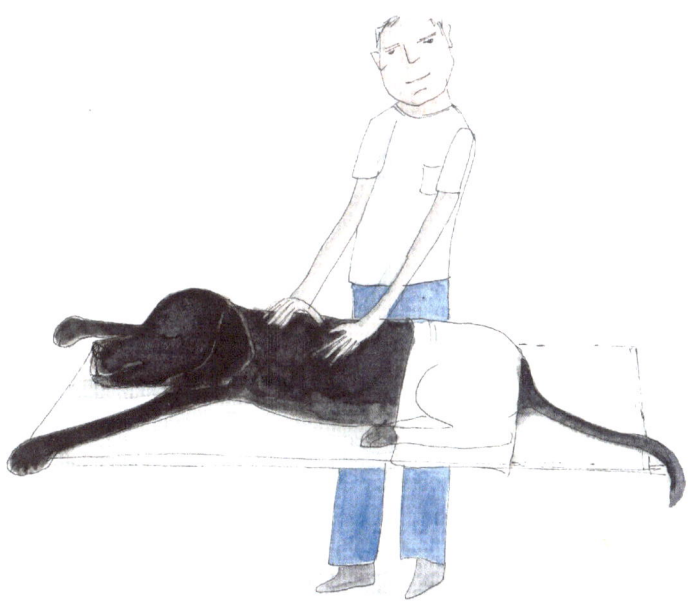

Indian head massage of ears, nose & throat
Essential oils rubbed into my coat
Manicure, pedicure, filed polished nails
Entitlement complex I had in spades
Attention given to my abs & my quads
Shoulders & neck, a decadent dog
Healing hands all down my spine to my hips
To my chinny chin chin Phil got to grips
This dark hairy chest & home to my heart
Round circular movements as blood vessels sparked
One's sense of wellbeing was Heaven sent
Henceforth my massage was a daily event

One day these therapies were stopped in their tracks
Old Jimmy Joe's slurry splutter splashed past
Nostrils winced in soft sensitive snout
Couldn't abide when the pig muck was out
Headed for cover in my basement bed
I budged not a jot, no matter what Fintan said
A protest sit in, abandon ship
When it came to slurry I shot from the hip
Gruesomely gassed two dark days at a time
Stank the dank washing that hung on the line
Choked small mammals as they ran for cover
Abomination of nature's mother

The Wind Up Merchant's Tail

The joker in the pack, that was me
Up to shenanigans with gusto & glee
Life with the Stauntons was pure fun & games
Worth the high risks & taking the blame
A real rapscallion daredevil dog
Rumplstiltskin, High Chieftain of the bog
The Snugborough Snuggler & none have surpassed
My supercalifragilistic goofs & gaffs
Dug up flower beds, slurped brews from their cups
I specialised in winding folks up
There was method in my animal madness you see
Laughter was medicine, still is and it's free

No one was safe when they called at my door
Big strong lungs & a bark like thunder roared
Black banshee lunged forth like a Baskerville
Firing on all cylinders by the windowsill
Women & children first were cuddle monstered
My charm offensive had them readily conquered
Full brute force as I launched hug attack
The strongest of men faltered & fell back
Sought ear rubs to get in; soft kisses to get out
All eyes to be on me whilst in my house
Grrrrreeetings were warm, "Chuck Mile Failte"
One hundred thousand welcomes never faltered

I was the children's pied piper of Hamlin
They saw magic in me as their favourite plaything
My little fans followed as I blazed a trail
Come rain, hail or shine we all chased my tail
At weekends I'd sit by every child's bed
Grabbed every duvet from over each head
Barks of delight as my victims emerged
Sleep-eyed, tongue-tied & softly snared
Excited laughter rang out through the air
I was their big black beautiful teddy bear
Doggy in their window with the waggliest tail
I'd hark "Bark Diem" & we seized the day

The Bark's Tail

Once upon a time in the olden days
One new arrival interrupted my play
A little brown box squealed with delight
High- pitched piercing sound gave my ears a fright
The village buzzed, we had a new neighbour
King Charles Spaniel? Do me a favour!
We had a monarch already –ME!
Top of the Snugborough family tree
My noble bloodline was pure and true blue
Harking right back to Brian Boru
High King of Eirean in ancient times
I told Charlie boy that Ireland was mine

The little chap was the smallest of dogs
No bigger than a sod of turf from the bog
The pampered pooch wore hand knitted jackets
Nipped ankles & yapped all day, what a racket
He ran under my feet to trip me up
Pinched my best biscuits the cheeky young pup
Little snub nose in the air high & haughty
Huge ego the size of Charlie Haughey
Big angel eyes disguised a mischievous soul
Enough was enough he just had to be told
So I took matters into my own paws
Cornered the blighter & laid down the law

Ever so gently I lifted him up
My soft velvet mouth had Charles by the scruff
Softly shaken but never once stirred
On not one occasion did I damage a hair
One simple lesson, show some respect
But who could have predicted what came next?
Net curtains twitched & my box was ticked
Charlie's crowd came down like a ton of bricks
Named, shamed & blamed "NOT GUILTY!" I barked
To new pastures in Partry I was dog marched
A new chapter in my life had just begun
What luck; I had two homes instead of just one

The Squire's Tail

So it once was one Saturday in spring
Lead, bowl & biscuits for Partry to bring
New move to "Lofthouse", abode of the Lowes
The warmest welcomes to me they would show
Arrived with Darragh in his old green van
Excited, wired, round & round their house I ran
Pushed my huge head through the patio doors
My giant frame followed, sheer size had them floored
With Labradorable spring in my step
New pastures in Partry, how good could it get?
Holidays in Snugborough there would always be
Indoors dog upgrade for semi-retired me

One family member was not at all pleased
She had been their only pet for years you see
Her name was Mixu (Mixed Up Cat With Lines On)
From her barbed wire claws I soon learned to run
She lay in wait at the foot of the stairs
Scratched, hissed & spat, caught this boy unawares
At every encounter my poor paws prayed
Yellow- eyed waspish stripes had my nerves frayed
Rattlesnake shake from the tip of her tail
My Chuck charm offensive just could not fail
If enemies caterwauled at her gates
My Black Panther pounce left all in its wake

Chipped away slowly at her fearsome moods
I became her protector, Sir. Chuck The Good
Offered my service as cuddly big brother
She swung from my tail, as I had with mother
Watched sunsets together under big Mayo skies
In our secret garden, Mixu & I
Raced & chased butterflies in warm summer meadows
As keen eyed kestrel watched high over hedgerow
Mixed Up Cat With Lines On & me were as one
Sphinx like we sat on our own grassy knoll
Lord & Lady of all we surveyed
Peace in our time reigned noble that day

The Postmistress's Tail

Letters & parcels mostly came through the post
The Vrrooom of the mail van thrilled me the most
Wheels crunched over gravel & then I would start
The howls of hell followed by bellowing bark
Jaws snapped & slavered then hackles were up
Freight train of furious fur, what a rush
Bull in a china shop barged the back door
Snatch & grab, five fingers could have been four
Postman to postmistress launched his complaint
Threat of police action frightened this saint
My case was pleaded over the dog & bone
Put under curfew from ten until one

This did not deter me one little bit
Obeyed my curfew but never would quit
Tall enough to scale kitchen tops
Swipe of my paw, post dropped into my chops
My letterbox jaws framed a big black hole
Most postal victims were gobbled down whole
Birthday & Christmas cards had not a chance
Tooth marked all with never a backwards glance
Devilishly good at devouring bills
Newspapers, magazines, maul overkill
Greedily grabbed at tax discs for the car
Sank teeth in & relished my new credit cards

Two telephone books proved a bridge too far
Took me seven hours & had to bite hard
Jiffy bags, parcel tags, catalogue bling
All manner of packaging tied up with string
Of course I was shouted at now & again
Gave them the sad eyes & took it like a man
There was no such thing as junk mail to me
No discrimination, gulped all with glee
It was such an irresistible urge
Obsessive-compulsive adrenalin surge
Brown & white envelopes airmailed on wings
Seized a good few of my favourite things

The Knight's Tail

It was on the night before Christmas Eve
And all through my snout season's eatings weaved
Supper was ready, so too were my guests
Roast Lamb all dressed up in its Sunday best
Guffaws of laughter, chink clunk of glass
"Is there room at The Village Inn?" they asked
"Be a good boy Chuck, stay back at the ranch"
Waved them off at the window & seized my chance
Mixed Up Cat With Lines On herself was out
My pack in the pub on their first pint of stout
Sly by the breakfast bar I sidled in
Decided then & there that who dares wins

I became Sir. Chuck, Knight of my own realm
Captain of this ship & proud at the helm
Within my rights & well entitled
To fine feasts & banquets of all I could snifle
Objects of my desire hid in bone china
Two legs of lamb big as ocean liners
Slavver chops in floods, eyes big as saucers
Gluttonous as the Franklin of Geoffrey Chaucer
Pawzer tank blistering blitzkrieg attack
Had lamb & china floored in a death throw crash
Carnivorous glare of Tyrannosaurus Rex
No prizes for guessing what came next?

Paws pounded ground, water trembled in glass
Earth shattering sound with each step I passed
Jagged edged jaw gnawed & ripped at pink flesh
Ferociously frenzied, a madman possessed
Dinnersaurus Rex, huge head raised & roared
No prisoners taken by this Labrador
Crescendo was reached at the witching hour
Not a scrap left, I had both beasts devoured
My great crusade clean up skills were exemplar
Worthy of the legendary Knights' Templar
But was this to be my condemned man's last meal?
Doe eyed charm offensive won on appeal

The Man of Paw's Tail

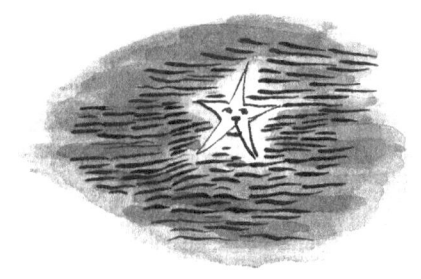

Each dog is blessed with four precious paws
Perfectly padded soft homes to his claws
Deftly designed to meet every terrain
Waterproofed tyres through thick mud & hard rain
God given foundations of my proud build
Four cornerstones for my earthly space to fill
Above them rose four fine columns of legs
Shiny black pillars, muscled sinews of strength
Joined at the hip, abridged across my chest
My north, my south, my east & my west
Torso & head balanced on four perfect plinths
Grand architecture demands the finest footprint

A canine spirit has everlasting light
Dog Star Sirius shines brightest in the night
When you thought you taught us to raise our paws
We hold them high anyway to dog bless you all
In troubled times when I soft pawed your knee
Compassionate love's understanding from me
In joyful times I would roll over Rover
All fours in the air high as super novas
My paws boasted four semi-webbed feet
From Springer spaniel mum should I the water meet
Black lab dad gave me giant aces of spades
Four lucky card feet from cradle to grave

These paws were the secret of my success
Kept me always four steps ahead of the rest
I became adept at opening doors
Swiped bacon butties from plate to the floor
Scratched the skirting boards for every last crumb
These claws manoeuvred all foods to my tum
They put my brakes on when outside the vet's
Abominable No Man had fight in me yet
My front paws were legend when grasping chew-sticks
Iron clad grip around mega marrowbones thick
Every dog's paw speaks his language by sign
Big happy high fives to all of mankind

The Ploughman's Tail

I was driven to Westport one fine day
To Old Head beach on the shores of Clew Bay
Soft sea salted air, warm sun overhead
Over white sands to crystal waters I was led
Ocean sprayed nostrils, wind wafted ears
Rippling with excitement, I was moved to tears
Rainbow clad kids, sand castled & ice creamed
Boys fished in rock pools beneath seagull screams
Tsunami-like wave as I dive bombed in
Went after sticks with a dog paddled swim
Blazed a wave of destruction in my wake
As all were chuckquaked by my coldwater shake

Back at the car, I was towelled & dried
Jumped into Land Rover for a joyride
My barks of delight boomed from the back seat
Off to the Shebeen for something to eat
Parked up & tied to the pub trestle table
Ordered to lie down & remain stable
Asked to guard Rosie as Simon went in
Wafts of sweet smells drifted out from within
Left his best friend & Rosie for food
Were we abandoned or was he just rude?
My incredible hulk was pea green with envy
 "FIE FOE FUM" this grub giant was frenzied

I smelled the blood of a turkey & ham
Enraged as I saw the Shebeen doors slam
Hatched a plan for the wood trestle table
Worthy of Aesop, a wrestled fable
Dogged determination followed my nose
Dragged trestle table, cider & Rosie
Adrenalin fuelled this big bad wolf ogre
Ploughed strong as an ox to mouth watering odours
My Samson strength was the stuff of folklore
True grit had got me to that Shebeen door
If you ever doubt your own inner strength?
Stout -hearted commitment scales life's highest fence

Why The Bath? The Tail

I had my share of trials & tribulations
Bath time had me all at battle stations
Torrential thunder clapped down from two taps
Was a watery grave in store for this chap?
The room with the bath was my temple of doom
Sinister steam clouds menacingly loomed
Toil troubled waters in hot cauldron bubble
I cut a tragic figure, this spelled trouble
Told cleanliness is next to dogliness
Religious fervour had me in a mess
My zealous pack were out on a mission
But this was the ultimate imposition

Elusive Scarlet Pimpernel was I
With ghostly premonition, was my end nigh?
Slunk around, tried to hide in dark corners
But was ten times the size of Little Jack Horner
My furrowed brow peered over patchwork quilt
Coaxed & cajoled, would my resolve wilt?
I gingerly tiptoed around the bed
Snatched wafer thin ham bribe & swiftly fled
Turned to cold stone by the bedside table
My noble struggle to remain stable
Battalions of bath's lotions & potions
Biblical deluge of epic proportions

At bathroom door I teetered on the brink
Dashed in & found refuge under the sink
Collar was off, my fear now intense
Psycho shower scene of Hitchcock suspense
Shrieks of delight at my predicament
Defeated I sighed & took my punishment
Cascades of suds loosened caked in mud
Escaped down the plughole, as I wished I could
Swung low, sweet harried hound, coming for to cringe in the foam
Sponged slow, heat lathered frown, running waters lone & forlorn
Revenge is best when served wet & cold
Drowned all soundly when I shook rattled & rolled

The Parson's Nose Tail

All roast chickens deserve a tail of their own
To parson's noses I dedicate this ode
A protuberance of sweet softened delight
Served with roast dinner on a cold winter's night
Tempting my taste buds, the seven deadly sins
In face of such forces, how could I win?
Prided myself on the hottest chicks in town
Envied all with full plates big & round
Wrath was incurred if the cat was fed first
Sloth like slumbers with my tum fit to burst
Gluttony & greed would come dine with me
Labrador food lust is legend you see

The sights & smells of slow roasted chicken
Basting beauties sure made my heart quicken
Honey glazed over & lemon juice squeezed
Sage & onion stuffing went down with ease
Skin crisped to perfection, succulent within
My taste buds' patience was sure wearing thin
From my chin charged a Niagara of falls
Lake Superior formed at the base of my claws
Fought back tears of joy as I reached my goal
Art of the alchemist, base meals turned gold
With quicksilver moves, I could not desist
Regarding roast chicken, these jaws never missed

Full Monty treatment had my plate destroyed
I was the personification of joy
Shook my tail feathers from the parson's nose
Prostrate by the fireside I struck a pose
In the bowels of the oven was left no scrap
Giblets & gravy filled this well fed chap
Mashed potatoes, butter blended & creamed
Brimmed full to burst in a bloat bellied dream
I counted on all the chickens that hatched
My conveyor belch devoured every batch
Chicken or egg, which came first you ask?
Supreme of chicken every time I laughed

The Honk's Tail

I was a Land Rover Discovery dog
Down highways & byways, a barking road hog
A Sunday spin would be top of my list
Bounded into my jeep, off I was whisked
Dry stonewalls we passed on our merry way
Headed for wild Atlantic coves & bays
Silver Strand beach, hound paradise found
White sands glistened bright for miles around
A beachside hostelry welcomed us in
Our seats in the stalls for tonics & gin
Ran hell for leather at sea air I gulped
Giant deep paw prints reflected my bulk

After my run & good stretch of the legs
Pub grub on tables had me put straight to bed
Risk stakes were high of my pilfering from plates
Bundled into Land Rover to keep lunch safe
First I lay down between the back two seats
But soon missing out on their friends' meet & greet
Two sets of couples sat down with my lot
The craic seemed mighty, the food piping hot
I was born to perform on centre stage
Me stuck in the car did not a good boy make
Enough was enough, something had to be done
Jumped into the driver's seat & parked my bum

Set my big bark at the top of its gears
Howling wolf broke sound barriers in ears
Paws clawed & scratch slashed at the dashboard
Full throttled fury, I would not be ignored
Dog breath steamed windows so none could see out
Cruising for a bruising, I threw my weight about
What did I have to do to gain attention?
Would I have to wait until my pension?
Guardian angels whispered over my shoulder
Suggested I should sit on the blower
Honked trumpet voluntary, all ears in traction
Battle of attrition won by rear guard action

The Physician's Tail

The physician's tail, a medicinal fable
I well remember his cold metal table
Mr. Conal Finnerty was a jovial bloke
Boisterous banter over ears, nose & throat
Every dog's life needs at the very least
A very good lawyer, physician & priest
Three wise men to follow me near & far
These noble kings orientated my star
Both lawyer & priest I needed the least
My veterinary physician often saved this beast
Check ups & boosters, thermometers in
To his Ballinrobe practice was brought this big 'yin

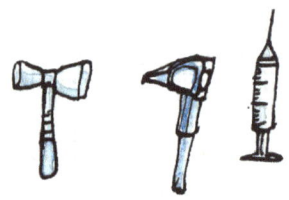

Vet's waiting rooms, the most anxious of places
Fearful expressions on patients' faces
Jumping Jack Russells could pose a huge threat
Feisty fellows whom upon you could set
Their sheer audacity belied their size
They packed a punch taking all by surprise
A heavyweight boxer entered the ring
Miniature poodle bedecked in her bling
Aristocats slinked in, two sleek Siamese
Feline fatales with high maintenance fees
My name was called for my turn to go in
All round the room an array of sly grins

My senior years proved a complex story
Many house calls kept me hunky & dory
Vitamin K shots if I grabbed grub outside
The threat of poison on my patch was high
Lotions & potions, powders & creams
Arthritis salts, antibiotics mean
Drugs of choice for this apothecary's dream
Eyes tested, claws clipped, ears dusted clean
Surgeries covered by pet insurance
Wore my lampshades with clumsy endurance
Thanks be to Conal & his veterinary team
Without whom I would not have seen sweet sixteen

The Pardon Me Tail

My vintage years had me hard of hearing
For Labradors, an unfortunate sure thing
In my young buck days all pitches of sound
Blasted through my headphones loud & proud
NASA space stations orbiting Earth
Their spy codes scrambled through my state secret work
007 had nothing on me
Black tie & tailcoat fit to a tee
Chauffer driven in my black Mercedes Benz
My face was my fortune it charmed foe & friend
State of the art gadgets stealthily hid
Heard all spies' thoughts & I knew were you lived

All the James Bonds, from Connery to Craig
Lacked charisma & chuckzpah that I displayed
Diamonds are forever strong & steadfast
I guarded the world to the very last
I had been in the finest of fettles
When sound receded, I grasped the nettle
A decade's Secret Service had been a rare treat
Time to retire to my three Shredded Wheat
I was the top dog of double agents
None could fill these paws my post remains vacant
Retired to pastures green with full field honours
Now that never happened to old Sean Connery

My hearing proved a common talking point
More trips to the vet as I girded my loins
Both black velvet wings were tested & screened
Torchlight & camera both intervened
Aging gracefully, sublime & serene
Some sounds were now fading from my scene
A blessing in disguise I was sure
Certain voices I no longer endured
A fluent lip reader & master of mime
My older dog learned new tricks all the time
In this small tail lies a message of hope
Through adversity, we adapt & we cope

The Cook's Tail

My favourite word just had to be cook
The best job ever by far in my book
Chef's hat & pinafore, ladle & spoon
Kitchen equipment had me all of a swoon
Scrip – scrape of knives whilst preparing to carve
Leg, wing & breast proved a game of two halves
Roast topside of beef blush pink at its heart
Horseradish at full gallop, pungent & tart
Scintillating smells from luscious lamb cutlets
Swashbuckled blaze of muzzle & muskets
Atlantic salmon in oceans of butter
At the hands of all that lot, I was mere putty

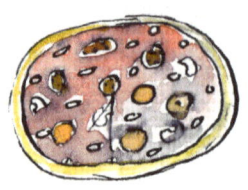

My role in this saga was that of Head Chef
Food was my sport I was linesman & ref
Kitchen persuits, my preferred playing field
Saucer's apprentice, oh the magic we weaved
Over cauldron aromas cast iron pan spells
Illuminating recipes, the book of smells
I used my powers like a hypnotist
Look into my eyes & none could resist
Taste tester supreme, a real steak shifter
Chairman of the chopping board of lobster bisquers
Canineoisseurs voted this top dog's dinner
The grand undisputed Master Shep Winner

Let us savour Saturday night takeaways
Hot boxes of booty took my breath away
I spied my pack's little eyes glued to menus
With touch of a glutton went smart phone to venue
Supermacs, indian, chinese or chipper?
I was no stranger to a chicken dipper
Stone baked or deep pan all lovingly cut
Had a domino effect on this pizza mutt
At crisp crusted crumbs jaws went like the clappers
Mozzarella meltdown the jowls of this snapper
Crowned & anointed High King of the kitchen
Head Chef Chuck earned my 3 stars from Michelin

The Manhandled Tail

My Simon & I one day did decide
To head for bog land for a duck & a dive
Whirling like a dervish I danced down my drive
A spinning top dog with a lust for life
Paws gathered pace, on the trail I was hot
Lead chain chimed time to my amble & trot
Our peace & tranquillity knew no bounds
Sweet sound of silence for Simon & hound
West of Ireland landscapes made me sigh
Shackles were off & so too was I
My bolt of black lightening blazed across the sky
With zigzag manoeuvre went my well-trained eye

Snout to ground with the finest of noses
Pheasant scent found, all coming up roses
Off went my hurricane in full hot persuit
Scent & search veteran of many a fine shoot
Keen as hot mustard with a fine tuned mind
I forgot all concepts of space & time
Ground gave way beneath I was stopped in my tracks
I avalanched down with a wallop bang splash
Dazed & confused as concussion set in
But who would notify my next of kin?
Spladooshed down ditch walls I thrashed & I scratched
For this force of gravitas I was no match

I heard my Duke of Wellingtons on mud
My guardian angel looked down from above
Simon, shining light at the end of my tunnel
With his escape plan in place, hope sprang eternal
He spread-eagled the land, brought me back from the dead
Launched this giant black rocket right over his head
I had been to the dark side of my own moon
Re-entry & splashdown could not come too soon
The world held its breath on my Chuck TV
Rescue mission worthy of Apollo 13
That day changed this boy's life like no other
Simon & Chuck fully bonded Mud Brothers!

The Miller's Tail

This tail acknowledges life's true flour power
Cometh the baker man cometh the hour
Our daily bread, the most ancient of foods
More essential to life than oil's finest crude
Its humble ingredients yield up pure gold
The strong staff of life for body & soul
Each nation on Earth bakes pride in its loaves
Born of all manner of ovens, fires & stoves
This world is one great continental breakfast
All creatures great & small in daily repast
Every household should have a breadwinner
The proud provider of every dog's dinner

It had to be said that I loved my bread
A freshly baked bun had me easily led
I could resist all things but temptation
One day proved to be a French Revelation
The sun was out, & so too was I
Above my head cotton clouds dotted blue sky
Al Fresco dining deemed order of the day
A feast for the senses was out on display
Cool cuts of meat posed with chilled rose wine
Out of my reach, but that was just fine
For I had just spied with my big brown eyes
The grandest French stick in the world, what a prize

My prey had fallen unnoticed in my path
Should I have told them? You were having a laugh
My fine French stick chick had warm golden skin
Full of wheaten promise, soft & chic within
A dress of fine white tissue clothed her curves
I positioned myself & held my nerve
Precision of movement with one fell swoop
Pierced her soft midriff then up she was scooped
Each half end hung either side of my jaws
My rear view receded as I quickened my paws
Rosie was screaming, "OFF WITH HIS HEAD!"
This dog had had his day...................and his daily bread

The Frankincense's Tail

This was the season to bark & be jolly
By home fires my basket bedecked with holly
Christmas stockings hung merrily on high
Santa Paws' sleigh rode through starlit night sky
This creature not stirring from hearth nor from house
Mixed Up Cat With Lines On out stalking a mouse
Post dinner lie down, this goose was getting fat
Full on Feast of Stephen went my King Wenceslas
Under the tree sat an army of presents
Season's eating's, a fine brace of pheasant
Tables & worktops well laden with food
Bright lanterns & tree lights enhanced my mood

Frankincensed air wafted over my head
Entrenched in my lair, I was warmed & fed
I was happy out with my wonderful life
Loved & adored with no stress & no strife
How could I have known from my fireside bed?
That the sword of Damocles hung over my head?
It's best not to know for whom the bell tolls
Ignorance is bliss when the dice of life roll
A good stretch of the legs saw me up on my feet
To dive bomb the sofa for big meets & greets
Brushed past the chimney breast as I took flight
Became a Roman candle as my tail set a-light

Screams of shock & awe at my perilous plight
Divine intervention was needed that night
Held down by Simon I was subdued & tamed
But tea towel attack only fanned my flames
Was I to become a towering inferno?
A spontaneous combustible nuclear glow?
Rosie made an inspired discovery
Threw wine like water, I was doused to recovery
The end of my tail looked sorry & charred
But not one inch of skin was burned or scarred
A Christmas miracle that night had occurred
Wine turned into water & this boy was spared

The Bin Beast's Tail

This saga captures my fatal attraction
To get down & dirty for a bit of bin action
Pedal & swing – recycle & wheelie
Disposal receptacles I loved sincerely
Refuse sacs to you are unwanted wastelands
To me bin lids were gateways to tasteland
Every week saw me fall down the grab it hole
Bin wonderland saw me dig for food's gold
Down black bin bag tunnel paw spades followed snout
Monster mole me was no mining slouch
Heaved up a Himalayan mountain of mess
What lay in my debris field was anyone's guess?

I scanned the scene with supernatural sight
Count Dracula dog in search of a bite
A delicatessen before me arrayed
Hidden gems & goodies randomly displayed
Dollops of sweet fat from Sunday's lamb roast
Half a sausage roll & odd bits of toast
Unwanted baked spud would find a good home
But lettuce & cucumber lowered the tone
Silver curry boxes sparkled & shone
This pirate fell for their spiced Siren song
An abandoned bagel packed with cream cheese
Fisherman's pie sailed into harbour with ease

I slunk away from the scene of my crimes
Food vacuumed clean, the inedible left behind
I was prime suspect, but no one could prove
Pointed paws at the cat on her hot bin roof
On the morning after the night before
The hair of this dog that bit bins was no more
I woke to see Rosie glaring down at me
My face no longer charmed the birds from the trees
This dastardly dog's guilt could no longer be hid
Head & shoulders surrounded by swing bin lid
High Court to Crimewatch my rogue's gallery found fame
Self-portraited Bin Beast, spectacularly framed

The Man of Love's Tail

Labradorables are love's embodiment
Angel hearts clothed in fur we're Heaven sent
The force is with us to light up dark skies
For where would we be without love in our lives?
We enable the disabled & guide the blind
Best nannies in the world for children you'll find
Our breed is adept at fighting crime
Our snouts sniff out drugs of the nastiest kind
Some of us sense the most sinister of cancers
An early warning bark to root out the canker
For narcoleptic children we raise house alarm
Disasters averted keeping everyone calm

Cupid's arrow randomly strikes at the heart
I was one such victim, gave me a start
A rare black beauty glided by my wall
Marcel waved Momo was supermodel tall
Heart skipped a beat, four legs turned to mush
Ashes to ashes & dust to dust
Enslaved, ensnared at first hurdle I fell
Her wicked witchery had me in trancelike hell
My huge heart hurt, love pangs cut like a knife
Labrador limpet clung on for dear life
I wolf howled up a cacophony of din
Chucked into Tom's van I was gone with the wind

Love comes to us all in many a guise
A kindness from a stranger, a word from the wise
The outstretched hand proffered in times of woe
Love lifts our wings to fly over that rainbow
The paw on your shoulder as I read your mind
These eyes that adored you so loyal & kind
I have Labradored all who crossed my paws' path
Twenty-two tails told in a barrel load of laughs
Plenty new to unfold in the fullness of time
Black magic muttlery spells more life & rhymes
It's hard hungry work bearing one's soul
We're going to need a bigger bowl

Epidogue

You have journeyed alongside this hairy hound
Let us stop for a breather & all gather round
Are you sitting comfortably? Then I'll begin
This summation of my shenanigans
Always at top table, living high on the hog
My quintessential food fiend of a dog
It is said that music is food for the soul
This Chuck Berry trail blazed his own Rock & Bowl
Dinnersaurus dog's Tyrannosaurus Rex
A bite to remember as good as it gets
Knight of the round table, Chuck the brave
Legend in my own knife time from ladle to gravy

From Snugborough to Partry we've traversed this read
Intrepid adventurers you followed my lead
A fine cast of players met on our way
Ms. Mixed Up Cat With Lines On made me pray
St. Simon beatified by this grateful dog
For a courageous rescue once upon a bog
My deadly piewayman at his black best
Binned & delivered an Everest of mess
A repeat offender sent down for life
Pincer movements worthy of Mack The Knife
Scythed through lamb cutlets all muzzle & muskets
Black belt in the art of master muttlery

But we'll meet again, don't know where & don't know when
Yes I know we'll mutt again some funny day
Keep smiling through just like you always do
Till our blue skies drive the bark cries faraway
So until then, these paws take to their pen
To write new tails from my secret Mayo den
Oh muttley crew, here's to lookin' at you
Kiss & missing you already toodaloo
Until I return, please bear hug this thought
Forget everything that you have been taught
Close your eyes tight shut & picture this buck
LABRACADABRA! In your mind's eye will be Chuck